CONQUISTADORS!

VALERIE BODDEN

CREATIVE EDUCATION · CREATIVE PAPERBACKS

CONQU

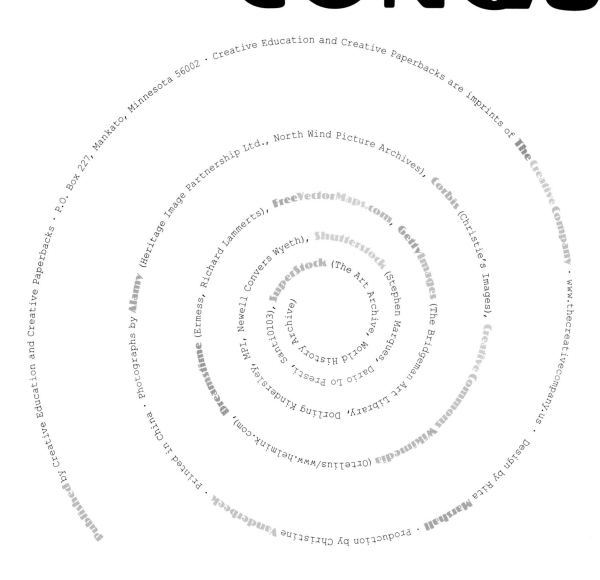

Published by Creative Education and Creative Paperbacks · P.O. Box 227, Mankato, Minnesota 56002 · Creative Education and Creative Paperbacks are imprints of The Creative Company · www.thecreativecompany.us

Design by Rita Marshall · production by Christine Vanderbeek · Printed in China

Photographs by Alamy (Heritage Image Partnership Ltd., North Wind Picture Archives), Corbis (Christie's Images), Creative Commons Wikimedia (Ortelius/www.helmink.com), Dreamstime (Ermess, Richard Lammerts), FreeVectorMaps.com, GettyImages (The Bridgeman Art Library, Dorling Kindersley, MPI, Newell Convers Wyeth), Shutterstock (Stephen Marques, Darío Lo Presti, sant0103), Superstock (The Art Archive, World History Archive)

Library of Congress Cataloging-in-Publication Data Names: Bodden, Valerie, author. • Title: Conquistadors / Valerie Bodden. • Series: X-Books: Fighters. • Includes bibliographical references and index. • Summary: A countdown of five of the most legendary conquistadors provides thrills as readers explore the lives, weapons, and battle tactics of these Spanish fighters. • IDENTIFIERS: LCCN 2016040243 / ISBN 978-1-60818-812-3 (HARDCOVER) / ISBN 978-1-62832-415-0 (PBK) / ISBN 978-1-56660-860-2 (EBOOK) • Subjects: LCSH: 1. America—Discovery and exploration—Spanish—Juvenile literature. 2. Conquerors—America—History—Juvenile literature. 3. Conquerors—Spain—History—Juvenile literature. • CLASSIFICATION: LCC E141.B644 2017 / DDC 970.01/6—dc23 • CCSS: RI.3.1-8; RI.4.1-5, 7; RI.5.1-3, 8; RI.6.1-2, 4, 7; RH.6-8.3-8
First Edition HC 9 8 7 6 5 4 3 2 1 • First Edition PBK 9 8 7 6 5 4 3 2 1

ISTADORS

CONTENTS

SLAVES

GOLD

LAND

SILVER

GOODS

} **GOALS OF CONQUEST**

XACTING FIGHTERS

In the early 1500s, conquistadors set out from Spain. They sailed for the New World across the sea. These extreme fighters were in search of riches and glory.

Conquistador Basics

Conquistadors came to the Americas from Spain. The word *conquistador* is Spanish for "conqueror." These conquerors wanted to take over the New World. They had heard stories of great riches there.

Conquistadors did not travel alone. They put together small armies. On early trips, the soldiers were paid a **salary**. Later, they were given a share of the riches they found.

MAP OF THE WORLD (1400s)

Until the 1500s, many people believed there were only three continents: Europe, Asia, and Africa.

MAP OF THE WORLD (PRESENT DAY)

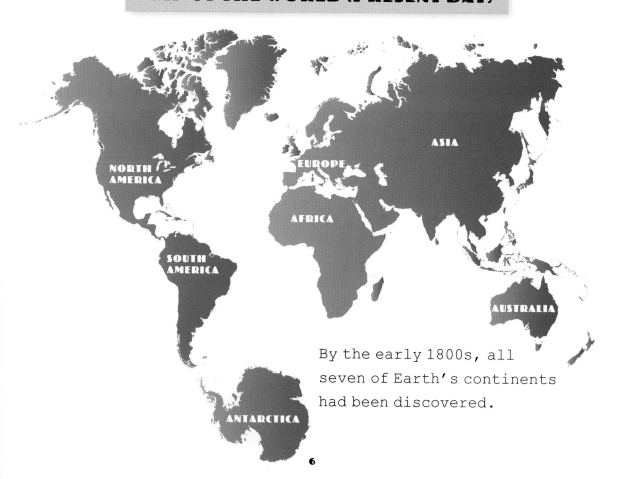

By the early 1800s, all seven of Earth's continents had been discovered.

THE PERIOD FROM THE 1400s TO THE 1600s IS KNOWN AS THE AGE OF DISCOVERY.

Explorers traveled the globe during this time.

They made detailed maps of new areas.

They searched for land, treasure, and trading partners.

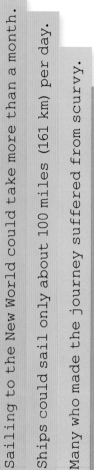

Sailing to the New World could take more than a month.

Ships could sail only about 100 miles (161 km) per day.

Many who made the journey suffered from scurvy.

They had open mouth sores and rotted teeth.

Many died on the way.

Getting rich was not the conquistadors' only goal. They also wanted to claim new lands for Spain. Many wanted to spread Christianity, too.

The conquistadors met many native peoples in the New World. They called the people Indians. The armies killed many of the Indians. Others died of diseases the Spaniards brought to the New World. The Indians' bodies couldn't fight off these diseases. The Spaniards also forced many Indians to become slaves.

Many soldiers joined conquistador armies.

EXPERIENCED FIGHTERS

Conquistador armies included men from Spain, Portugal, Greece, France, and other countries.

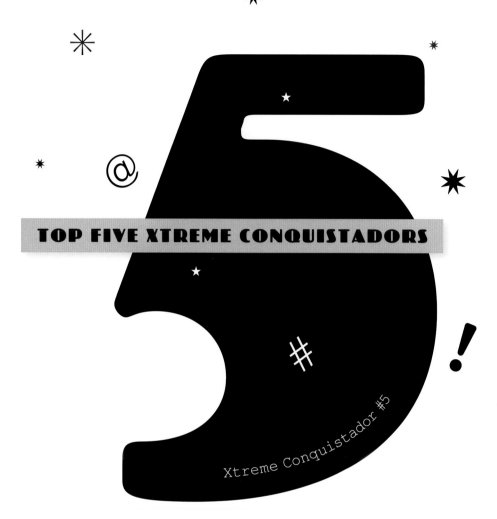

Xtreme Conquistador #5

Francisco de Orellana helped conquer the Incas of Peru. Afterward, he joined a group traveling to Ecuador. The group was led by Gonzalo Pizarro. Along the way, Orellana and Pizarro split up. Orellana and his men set out down a mighty river. They suffered hunger, illness, and Indian attacks. After seven months, they finally reached the sea. They were the first European explorers to travel the Amazon River.

Tales of conquistadors spread throughout Spain and the New World. Today, the names of the fiercest conquistadors are still remembered.

Life as a Conquistador

Many conquistadors sailed to South America. There they trekked hundreds of miles inland. The jungles of the New World were thick. They had to cut trails with swords and **machetes**. Horses, llamas, or slaves carried their supplies. Sometimes the conquistadors had to cross high, rocky mountains. When they came to rivers, they had to build bridges.

The jungles were hot and **humid**. During the wet season, it rained every day. In the mountains, there were snowstorms.

Sometimes the conquistadors ran out of food. They survived on snakes, shellfish, and other wild foods. Some even had to eat their horses.

Many conquistadors got sick from New World diseases. Others were killed by poisonous snakes. Some conquistadors got lost. They were never seen again.

Christopher Columbus
1492

sails to the New World

Ferdinand Magellan
1521

sails across the Pacific

sees the Pacific Ocean

Vasco Núñez de Balboa
1513

conquers the Aztec empire   conquers the Incan empire   temporarily bans conquests

1521
Hernán Cortés

1532
Francisco Pizarro

King Charles V
1550

LIFE AS A CONQUISTADOR FACT

Conquistador supplies at sea included food

such as salt, grain, and biscuits.

Xtreme Conquistador #4

Álvar Núñez Cabeza de Vaca In 1527, Cabeza de Vaca joined a conquistador army traveling to North America. The ship was wrecked in a storm. Cabeza de Vaca ended up in Texas. Local Indians made him a slave. He spent the next several years living with the Indians. Then he met up with three other survivors of the shipwreck. The men hiked 2,000 miles (3,219 km) to Mexico. They had been gone eight years.

XCESSIVE BATTLE

Conquistadors carried guns, swords, and crossbows. Their own armor was too heavy for conditions in the New World. So they adopted the armor of the Indians.

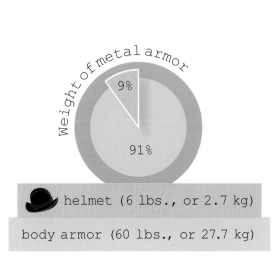

Weight of metal armor

9%

91%

helmet (6 lbs., or 2.7 kg)

body armor (60 lbs., or 27.7 kg)

CONQUISTADOR WEAPONS FACT

Spanish crossbows could launch a bolt up to 500 yards (457 m).

Conquistador Weapons

The conquistadors' heaviest weapons were cannons.
The cannons were usually mounted on ships. They could
also be strapped onto carts. Then they could be pulled
across land.

Many conquistadors carried a gun called a
harquebus. Others shot crossbows. For up-close
fighting, they used rapiers. These were thin, sharp
swords. Conquistadors on horses carried a broadsword.
This wide sword was swung with two hands.

In Spain, many soldiers wore metal armor. But
this kind of armor was hot and heavy. It made it
difficult to move through the thick jungles. So the
conquistadors used Indian armor. This armor was made
of hardened cotton. It was light and flexible. But
it could stop arrows and other Indian weapons. Many
conquistadors still wore their iron helmets.

XPLOSIVE TACTICS FACT

Indians had never seen guns or cannons before.

The sounds the weapons made scared them.

XPLOSIVE TACTICS

Conquistador armies were usually much smaller than Indian armies. But the Spaniards had better weapons. They often won the battle.

The atlatl was an Indian device used to throw spears. It could launch spears farther and harder than they could be thrown by hand.

GUN **CROSSBOW** **SWORD**

A conquistador army was divided into groups. Each group used a different weapon. One group fired guns. Another shot crossbows. A third wielded swords. The Spaniards had a well-trained cavalry, too. These soldiers fought from horseback. A soldier on a horse was harder for Indians on foot to reach.

A force of 100 Spaniards might take on thousands of Indians. The conquistadors were brutal in battle. They wiped out thousands of Indian warriors. They killed women and children, too. They tortured chiefs to get gold. Sometimes, they burned people or fed them to dogs.

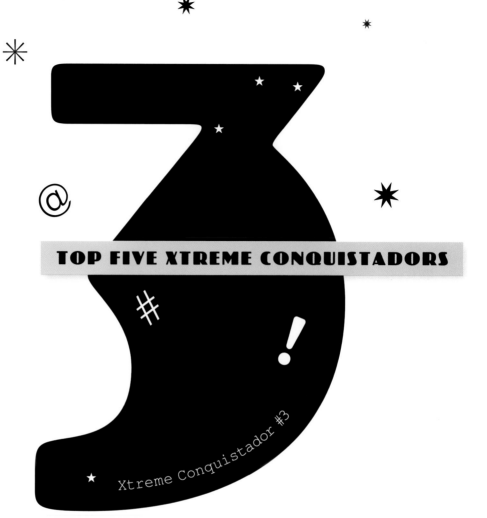

3

TOP FIVE XTREME CONQUISTADORS

Xtreme Conquistador #3

Pedro de Alvarado was known for his cruelty. He killed women and children. He destroyed villages. He fed Indians to his dogs. Alvarado was part of the army that conquered the Aztecs. He ordered an attack on the Aztecs as they celebrated a festival. Later, Alvarado conquered the Mayan people of Guatemala. He became governor there. But he continued to go on conquests. He died in a battle in 1541.

XTENSIVE LEGACY

Conquistadors roamed the Americas for 50 years. By the 1550s, fewer conquistadors explored the New World. Much of South America was then ruled by Spain.

Conquistador Legacy

The mighty Aztec and Incan empires had been destroyed by 1550. Other Indian peoples were nearly wiped out. But those who remained held on to their customs. Many traditions are still observed in South America today.

During their time, conquistadors were treated as heroes in Europe. People admired their bravery. Today, some people still admire conquistadors. Others see them as villains. They say the conquistadors destroyed a way of life. There is no question that they changed the New World forever. Their complicated legacy lives on.

Some conquistadors returned to Spain.

Many remained in the New World.

They became farmers or ranchers.

Others led new expeditions in North America.

The Spanish influence can still be seen in the Americas today. Spanish-style buildings are found across both continents. Christianity is the leading religion, largely thanks to the priests who traveled with and followed the conquistadors, spreading a form of Christianity known as Catholicism. And spanish is the national language of most of Central and South America.

About 250,000 Spaniards settled in the Americas in the 1500s.

TOP FIVE XTREME CONQUISTADORS

Xtreme Conquistador #2

Francisco Pizarro fought for the Spanish army. Then he traveled to the New World. There, he heard about the great riches of the Inca Empire. In 1531, he put together a force of 180 men. He led them through the jungles of Peru. His soldiers killed at least 2,000 Incas in 1532. They killed the Incan king, too. Pizarro set up the city of Lima. It is still the capital of Peru.

Conquistadors' ships were called caravels. They had two or three masts with triangle-shaped sails.

Many conquistadors searched for El Dorado, a legendary city of gold.

Some Indians made **alliances** with the Spaniards. They wanted their help to defeat enemy tribes.

Many Indian slaves were forced to work in mines or on **plantations**.

When their food ran out, one conquistador army ate their leather boots.

Indians sometimes used captured Spaniards as human sacrifices.

Spanish ships had special harnesses to hold horses still during the long ocean journey.

Cannons could blast a cannon ball more than 1.1 miles (1.8 km).

Some conquistadors used a halberd. This was a cross between a spear and an ax.

Spanish broadswords could be three feet (0.9 m) long.

Indians used arrows, swords, or clubs edged with glass against the conquistadors.

Indian armor was made by dipping woven cotton into salt water and letting it dry.

Gold and silver from the New World made Spain the richest country in the world.

The conquistador Vasco

Núñez de Balboa was the first European to see the eastern Pacific Ocean.

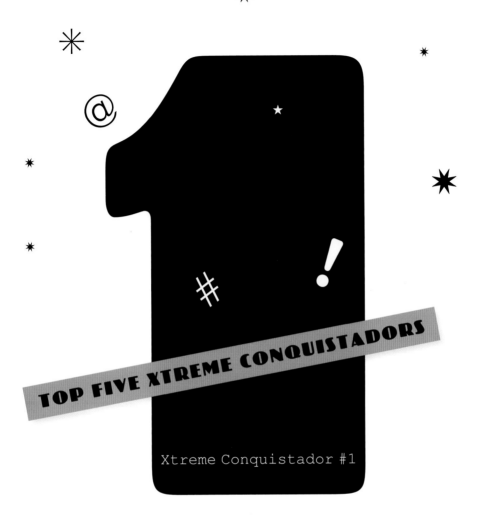

TOP FIVE XTREME CONQUISTADORS

Xtreme Conquistador #1

Hernán Cortés was one of the first conquistadors. He remains the best known. Cortés arrived in the New World in 1504. In 1519, he gathered 500 soldiers. Then he set sail for Mexico. He entered the land of the Aztecs. After several battles, the Aztecs surrendered in August 1521. Cortés set up a Spanish colony on their land. He called it New Spain.

GLOSSARY

alliances – agreements in which two or more groups of people agree to work together and help each other

humid – having a lot of moisture in the air

machetes – big, heavy knives used as weapons or to cut large plants

plantations – large farms for raising crops of plants or trees

salary – payment given to a person in return for doing work

RESOURCES

Dor-Ner, Zvi. *Columbus and the Age of Discovery*. New York: William Morrow, 1991.

PBS. "Conquistadors." http://www.pbs.org/conquistadors/index.html.

Thomas, Hugh. *World without End: Spain, Philip II, and the First Global Empire*. New York: Random House, 2015.

Wood, Michael. *Conquistadors*. Berkeley: University of California Press, 2000.

INDEX

Conquistadors saw animals, such as bison, that were unfamiliar to them.